Vegan Slow Cooker Recipes

125 Quick and Easy Vegan Slow Cooker Recipes that Taste Delicious

By Jennifer Ellis

Table of Contents

Introduction

Choosing to live the Vegan lifestyle is not just a trend. It's an important choice than many people make for a variety of reasons including weight loss, increased energy, clear skin, disease prevention and better health.

Whether you're only on a Vegan diet or a full lifestyle Vegan that refrains from using animal products in cosmetics and clothing, you'll undoubtedly have to make some sacrifices along the way. Yet you can still eat tasty and nutritious meals with minimal effort using your slow cooker.

In Vegan Slow Cooker Recipes, you'll find 125 delicious recipes including appetizers, breads, breakfasts, beverages, soups, stews, main dishes, side dishes, desserts, sauces and spreads. If you want a shortcut to great tasting Vegan meals, use this book as your guide for new and exciting Vegan slow cooker recipes that are quick and easy to prepare.

If you're tired of spending hours on Vegan food prep, it's time get started on your brand new path to Vegan slow cooker cooking!

Teriyaki Mushrooms

Ingredients:

5-6 cups small mushrooms, stems removed
2 cups teriyaki sauce
2 cups water
2 TBSP olive oil
1 cup raw honey
½ tsp pepper
¼ tsp ginger

Directions:

Place mushrooms in the slow cooker and put remaining ingredients on top. Stir to combine. Cover and cook on low for 6 hours, stirring occasionally.

Pumpkin Pie Dip

Ingredients:

2 cups pumpkin puree
1 cup cashew cream
2 TBSP almond butter
2 tsp pumpkin pie spice
1 tsp vanilla extract
¼ cup honey

Directions:

Combine all ingredients in your slow cooker and stir until completely mixed. Cover and cook on low for 1-2 hours. Serve with gingersnaps or apple slices.

Sweet and Sour Tofu

Ingredients:

1 lb extra firm tofu
2 TBSP canola oil
1 TBSP cornstarch
½ yellow onion, chopped
1 yellow bell pepper
1 cup broccoli florets
1 cup carrots, sliced
1 cup sliced water chestnuts
10 oz. sweet and sour sauce

Directions:

Press moisture out of the tofu and cut into bite size cubes. Coat the cubes with cornstarch and then fry in a canola oil for about 15 minutes or until crunchy on the outside. Place tofu and vegetables in your slow cooker and cover with sweet and sour sauce. Stir together and cover. Cook on low for 3 hours.

Sweet and Spicy Pecans

Ingredients:

1/4 cup coconut oil
6 cups pecans
2 tsp chili powder
2 tsp sugar
½ tsp cinnamon

Directions:

Heat the coconut oil in your slow cooker on high for 15 minutes or until melted. Pour in the pecans and stir until they are coated in the melted oil. Cover and cook on high for two hours. Then take the lid off the slow cooker and continue cooking on high for 2 ½ more hours, stirring every half hour. Sprinkle seasonings on top and spread on a baking sheet to cool.

Eggplant Hummus

Ingredients:

1 eggplant
2 garlic cloves
Juice from 1 lemon
2 TBSP sesame paste
1 TBSP dried parsley
Salt and pepper to taste

Directions:

Wash the eggplant and poke with a fork 4-5 times. Place it in the slow cooker and cover. Cover on high for 3 hours. Using tongs, remove the eggplant and cut it in half. Scrape out the seeds and discard. Now use a spoon to scoop out the flesh and place it in your blender with remaining ingredients. Puree until smooth.

Wasabi Almonds

Ingredients:

1 pound raw almonds
1 TBSP water
1 TBSP soy sauce
2 TBSP coconut oil, melted
2 TBSP wasabi powder
1 tsp salt

Directions:

Whisk together melted coconut oil, water, and soy sauce in a bowl. Pour in the almonds and toss to combine. Pour the almonds in a large zip-top bag and add in seasonings. Shake it to coat the almonds evenly. Now pour the almonds into your slow cooker and cover. Cover on low for 2-4 hours or until the almonds are toasted and lightly browned. Spread the almonds on a baking sheet and allow them to dry.

Creamy Vegetable Dip

Ingredients:

1/4 head of cauliflower
2 TBSP sesame paste
½ clove garlic
Juice from ½ lemon
1/8 cup water
1 TBSP olive oil
½ tomato, diced
Salt and pepper to taste
1 cup vegetable broth

Directions:

Place cauliflower and vegetable broth in slow cooker and cook on low for 4 hours. Then place cauliflower in your food processor with remaining ingredients and pulse until smooth.

Southern Boiled Peanuts

Ingredients:

2 pounds raw peanuts, in shell
¾ cup salt
12 cups water

Directions:

Combine all ingredients in the slow cooker and cover.
Cook on high for 18 hours or until peanuts are soft.
Drain and serve warm or store in refrigerator.

Vegan Chili Con Queso

Ingredients:

16 oz. cashew cream or other cream cheese substitute
4 cups meatless chili
½ cup chopped green chilies
1 jar of salsa
1 red onion, minced

Directions:

Combine all ingredients in the slow cooker and cover. Cook on high for one hour. Stir well before serving.

Slow Cooker Salsa

Ingredients:

10 tomatoes, cored and chopped
2 garlic cloves, minced
1 onion, chopped
2 jalapeno peppers, chopped
½ tsp salt
½ tsp cayenne pepper
¼ cup cilantro leaves, chopped

Directions:

Combine all ingredients except cilantro in slow cooker. Cover and cook on high for 1 hour or until you reach desired consistency. Stir in cilantro and serve with tortilla chips.

Rosemary Olive Oil Bread

Ingredients:

3 ½ cups all purpose flour
1 packet dry active yeast
1 ¼ cups warm water
¼ cup fresh rosemary, chopped, divided
3 TBSP olive oil
1 tsp sugar
1 tsp sea salt, divided

Directions:

In a large bowl, combine water, yeast, and sugar. Allow it sit and proof for 10 minutes. It will look foamy when it's ready. Stir in ½ tsp Salt, ½ of rosemary, 3 TBSP olive oil, and all of the flour. Mix until completely combined. Use your hands to form the dough if necessary. Grease a large bowl and place dough inside. Cover with a kitchen towel and leave in a warm area for one hour to rise. Remove the dough and roll into a ball. Allow it sit for another 20 minutes for the second rise. Turn your slow cooker on high and line it with two pieces of parchment paper, allowing a few inches to hang out on the sides of the slow cooker. Lay dough inside the slow cooker and sprinkle with salt and remaining rosemary.

Cover and cook for two hours. Then lift it out of the slow cooker and allow to cool. For a crunchier crust, place under the broiler for around 3 minutes.

Pumpkin Bread

Ingredients:

1 can of pumpkin puree (15 oz)
½ cup vegetable oil
½ cup sugar
½ cup packed brown sugar
1 ½ cups flour
¼ tsp Salt
1 tsp pumpkin pie spice
1 tsp baking soda
1 banana, pureed

Directions:

In a large bowl, beat together oil, sugar, and brown sugar. Stir in the pureed banana and pumpkin. Add remaining ingredients and mix to combine. Pour batter into a well greased bread pan. Add two cups of water to the slow cooker and lay the pan inside. Cover the top of the slow cooker with 8-10 paper towels to keep condensation from dripping down onto the bread. Place the lid on top and cook on high for 2 ½ to 3 hours or until a toothpick comes out clean.

Chocolate Chip Zucchini Bread

Ingredients:

1 cup applesauce
1 ½ cups sugar
3 cups flour
1 tsp baking soda
½ tsp baking powder
2 tsp cinnamon
3 tsp vanilla
¼ tsp Salt
2 cups peeled and grated zucchini
1 cup Vegan chocolate chips
1 ½ bananas, pureed (or other substitute for 3 eggs)

Directions:

Spray a 3-qt. slow cooker with non-stick spray. In a large mixing bowl, combine pureed banana, sugar, and applesauce. Next, stir in flour, baking powder, baking soda, cinnamon, Salt, and vanilla. Last, mix in zucchini and fold in chocolate chips. Pour batter into the slow cooker. Cook on low for 2-3 hours or until toothpick comes out clean. Flip onto a plate and allow to cool before slicing.

Apple Bread

Ingredients:

1 ½ cups Bisquick or other baking mix
½ cup coconut milk
1 cup apple pie filling
¼ cup vegetable oil

Directions:

Mix together bisquick, coconut milk, and oil. Stir in apple pie filling and then pour batter into your greased slow cooker. Cook on high for 1 hour to 1 ½ hours. It's done when a toothpick inserted in the center comes out clean.

Apricot Nut Bread

Ingredients:

1 cup all purpose flour
½ cup whole wheat flour
2 tsp baking powder
¼ tsp baking soda
½ tsp Salt
½ cup sugar
¾ cup almond milk
¼ cup vegetable oil
¾ cup dried apricots, chopped
1 TBSP grated orange peel
1 cup walnuts, chopped

Directions:

Combine dry ingredients in a large bowl. Add in almond milk, oil, and orange peel. Stir to combine. Fold in apricots and walnuts and pour into a well greased bread pan. Place on a rack in the slow cooker and cover, leaving a little room for steam to escape. Cook on high for 4-6 hours.

Slow Cooker Amish White Bread

Ingredients:

1 packet fast acting yeast
2 TBSP sugar
½ tsp salt
1 ½ cups flour
½ cup hot water (not boiling)
1 TBSP oil

Directions:

Combine yeast, sugar, salt, and flour in a large bowl, Slowly add in water and oil until dough forms. Form into a bowl and place in a greased bowl. Cover with a towel and allow to rise in a warm place for 1 hour or until doubled in size. Line slow cooker with parchment paper and place dough inside. Cover and cook on low for 1 ½ to 2 hours.

Whole Wheat Bread

Ingredients:

1 TBSP yeast
¼ cup warm water
1 cup warm almond milk
¼ cup rolled oats
1 tsp Salt
2 TBSP olive oil
2 TBSP raw honey
½ banana, mashed
¼ cup milet
2 TBSP ground flax seed
2 ¾ cup whole wheat flour

Directions:

In a large bowl, dissolve yeast in warm water and allow to proof for 10 minutes. It is done when it is bubbly and foamy on top. Add in remaining ingredients to form a dough and then knead for 5 minutes, until smooth and elastic. Place prepared dough into a greased bread pan. Add 1 cup water to your slow cooker and place bread pan on top. Cover and bake on high for 3 hours. Crack slow cooker to allow steam to vent if you notice condensation collecting on top.

Orange Cranberry Bread

Ingredients:

1 cup all purpose flour
½ cup whole wheat flour
2 tsp baking powder
¼ tsp baking soda
½ tsp Salt
½ cup sugar
¾ cup almond milk
¼ cup vegetable oil
¾ cup dried cranberries, chopped
2 TBSP grated orange peel
1 cup walnuts, chopped

Directions:

Combine dry ingredients in a large bowl. Add in almond milk, oil, and orange peel. Stir to combine. Fold in cranberries and walnuts and pour into a well greased bread pan. Place on a rack in the slow cooker and cover, leaving a little room for steam to escape. Cook on high for 4-6 hours.

Breakfast Risotto

Ingredients:

3 gala apples, chopped
1 ½ tsp cinnamon
1/8 tsp nutmeg
1/8 tsp cloves
¼ tsp Salt
¼ cup coconut oil
1/3 cup brown sugar
1 ½ cups Arborio rice
3 cups apple juice
1 cup almond milk

Directions:

Turn your crock to high and add the coconut oil so it can start melting. Chop apples while you wait. Stir in the rice to the coconut oil, then add apples and remaining ingredients. Cover and cook on high for 5 hours or low for 6-7 hours.

Cranberry Fig Oatmeal

Ingredients:

1 cup steel cut oats
1 cup dried cranberries
1 cup dried figs
4 cups water
1/2 cup almond milk

Directions:

Combine all ingredients in the slow cooker and stir to combine. Cover and cook on low for 8 to 9 hours.

Apple Walnut Oatmeal

Ingredients:

1 cup steel cut oats
1 cup chopped apples
1 cup chopped walnuts
4 cups water
1/2 cup almond milk

Directions:

Combine all ingredients in the slow cooker and stir to combine. Cover and cook on low for 8 to 9 hours.

Peaches and Cream Breakfast Cereal

Ingredients:

1 1/4 cups steel cut oats
1 can peaches, diced
1 cup chopped walnuts
4 cups water
1 cup coconut milk

Directions:

Combine all ingredients in the slow cooker and stir to combine. Cover and cook on low for 8 to 9 hours.

Cinnamon Applesauce

Ingredients:

3 1/2 lbs granny smith apples, peeled, cored, and sliced
1/2 cup packed brown sugar
1 1/2 TBSP fresh lemon juice
1/4 tsp ground cinnamon

Directions:

Combine all ingredients in the slow cooker and cook on high for 3 hours or on low for 5-6 hours. Mash with a potato masher and serve warm.

Pumpkin Spice Steel Cut Oats

Ingredients:

1 1/2 cup steel cut oats
4 cups water
1/8 cup pumpkin puree
1 tsp pumpkin pie spice
1 TBSP brown sugar
1 TBSP sugar

Directions:

Combine all ingredients in the slow cooker and stir to combine. Cover and cook on low for 8-9 hours.

Morning Plum Pudding

Ingredients:

2 cups dried, pitted plums
water to cover prunes
2/3 cup boiling water
1 cup raw honey
Zest from ½ orange
¼ cup almonds, chopped

Directions:

Soak the plums in water overnight. Take them out of the water and put in slow cooker. Add in 2/3 cup boiling water, honey, and orange zest. Cover and cook on high for 3 hours. Pour the plum pudding in a serving dish and chill for at least 2 hours. Top with chopped almonds and serve.

Warm Spiced Fruit

Ingredients:

3 cups sliced peaches
1 can pineapple tidbits with liquid
3 cups pear slices
½ cup green seedless grapes, halved
½ cup maraschino cherries, halved
1 ½ tsp cinnamon
1 tsp nutmeg
½ cup honey
4 TBSP coconut oil
½ cup coconut milk

Directions:

Combine all ingredients in the slow cooker and cover. Cook on low for 4-6 hours. Serve with whipped coconut cream if desired.

Vegan Breakfast Casserole

Ingredients:

5 cups frozen hash browns
2 cups cheese substitute
1 1/2 cups almond milk
½ cup chives
1 cup frozen peas
1 tsp salt
1 tsp pepper
1 tsp paprika

Directions:

Combine all ingredients in the slow cooker. Cover and cook on low for 6-8 hours.

Banana Bread Quinoa

Ingredients:

1 cup of quinoa
1 cup almond milk
1 tsp vanilla extract
1 cup water
1 1/2 banana (past ripe), mashed
2 tablespoons chopped walnuts
3 tablespoons brown sugar
1 1/2 tablespoons coconut oil, melted

Directions:

In a small bowl, mix the brown sugar and walnuts together. Pour quinoa, almond milk, water, butter and vanilla into the crock pot. Add the mashed banana and stir to evenly distribute. Sprinkle the sugar and walnut mixture into the quinoa and stir to combine. Cover and cook on low for 4-6 hours. Add additional almond milk as needed and add sugar to taste.

Breakfast Burrito Filling

Ingredients:

1 15oz can black beans, drained and rinsed
1 10oz can diced tomatoes with green chiles, don't drain
1 cup uncooked pearl barley
2 cups vegetable broth
¾ cups frozen corn
¼ cup chives
Juice from 1 lime
1 tsp ground cumin
1 tsp chili powder
½ tsp red pepper flakes
3 garlic cloves, minced

Directions:

Combine all ingredients in the slow cooker and cook on low for 5-6 hours. Place the filling inside warm tortillas for an instant breakfast burrito.

Baked Stuffed Apples

Ingredients:

6 large green apples
¼ cup raisins
¼ cup honey
1 tsp cinnamon
6 TBSP coconut oil

Directions:

Core apples, but leave about half an inch at the bottom. Divide raisins, honey, cinnamon, and coconut oil between the apples, stuffing the cavity where apples were cored. Placed stuffed apples in the slow cooker with ½ inch of water. Cook on low overnight.

Cherry Almond Granola

Ingredients:

5 cups old fashioned rolled oats
1 cup whole almonds
1/2 cup dried cherries
1/2 cup pepitas
1/4 cup shredded coconut
1/4 cup canola oil
1/4 cup honey
1 tsp vanilla

Directions:

Add the oats, honey, oil, almonds, and vanilla to the slow cover. Cook uncovered on high for one hour, stirring every 20 minutes. Reduce heat to low and add coconut, pepitas, and cherries. Cook on low uncovered for 4 more hours, stirring every half hour. Cook on baking sheets.

Mulled Apple Cider

Ingredients:

1 gallon apple cider
1/8 cup brown sugar
5 cinnamon sticks
1/4 tsp ground cloves
1/2 tsp ground nutmeg

Directions:

Combine ingredients in the slow cooker and cook on low for 2-3 hours.

Spiced Pumpkin Chai Tea

Ingredients:

4 cups almond milk
1 ½ cups brewed black tea
4 TBSP pumpkin puree
4 TBSP sugar
1 tsp pumpkin spice
2 tsp vanilla extract

Directions:

Whisk together all ingredients in slow cooker and cook on low for 2-3 hours. Serve with whipped coconut cream and a sprinkle of cinnamon on top.

Autumn Citrus Cider

Ingredients:

2 quarts apple cider
1 cup orange juice
½ cup lemon juice
¼ cup honey
8 whole cloves
3 slices ginger
3 cinnamon sticks, broken into pieces

Directions:

Place spices in a spice bag made from cheesecloth and tie shut. Pour apple cider, orange juice, lemon juice, and honey into the slow cooker and stir to combine. Add in spice bag. Cook on low for 5-6 hours. Remove spice bag and serve.

Mulled Cranberry Punch

Ingredients:

Juice from 1 orange
8 cups cranberry juice
1 ½ cups white grape juice concentrate
½ cup raspberries
2 cups water
2 cinnamon sticks, broken
8 whole cloves
4 whole allspice

Directions:

Place spices in a spice bag made from cheesecloth and
tie shut. Pour orange juice, cranberry juice, grape juice
concentrate, water, and raspberries into the slow
cooker. Stir to combine. Add spice bag and cover. Cook
on low for 4-6 hours. Remove spice bag and serve.

Vegan Hot Cocoa

Ingredients:

4 cups coconut milk
1/3 cup sugar
1/3 cup cocoa powder
1 tsp vanilla extract
Dash of salt
Dash of cinnamon

Directions:

Whisk together ingredients in the slow cooker until well combined. Heat on high for 1-2 hours. Stir and serve immediately.

Spiced Holiday Punch

Ingredients:

4 cups cranberry juice
4 cups pineapple juice
1/3 cup red hots candy
1 cinnamon stick

Directions:

Combine all ingredients in the slow cooker and cook on
low for 4-5 hours. Stir and serve immediately.

Gingerbread Latte

Ingredients:

4 cups coconut milk
1/2 cup white sugar
2 tsp ground ginger
2 tsp vanilla extract
1 tsp ground cinnamon
1/4 tsp cloves
1/4 tsp nutmeg
1/2 cup strong black coffee, or a freshly-brewed shot of espresso

Directions:

Combine all ingredients except coffee in the slow cooker. Cover and cook on low for 3 hours. Pour over a cup of strong black coffee or espresso. Garnish with whipped coconut cream if desired.

Winter Wassail

Ingredients:

2 quarts apple cider
½ cup orange juice
1 cup pineapple juice
1/2 cup honey
3 sticks cinnamon
2 whole cloves
1 whole orange, cut in rings

Directions:

Combine all ingredients in the slow cooker, allowing orange rings to float on top. Cover and cook on low for 4 hours. Serve immediately.

Peppermint Mocha

Ingredients:

4 cups coconut milk
1/3 cup sugar
1/3 cup cocoa powder
1 tsp vanilla extract
6 peppermint candies
Strong black coffee or espresso

Directions:

Whisk together ingredients in the slow cooker until well combined, allowing peppermint candies to sink to the bottom. Heat on high for 1-2 hours. Pour over ½ cup strong black coffee or espresso. Garnish with a candy cane in each mug.

Kale Soup

Ingredients:

1 head kale, washed and chopped
1 large can crushed tomatoes
1 can chickpeas
1 can red beans
1 can white beans
4 carrots, peeled and sliced into rounds
3 stalks celery, chopped
1 yellow onion, diced
Salt and Pepper to Taste
1 cup vegetable stock
1 cup water

Directions:

Add all ingredients to your slow cooker and stir just to combine. Cook on low for 8-10 hours.

Golden Onion Soup

Ingredients:

12 cups vegetable broth
1 yellow onion, sliced
5 button mushrooms, sliced thin
2 stalks celery, diced
½ cup chives
Salt and pepper to taste

Directions:

Place all ingredients in your slow cooker and cook on low for 4 hours.

White Bean Chili

Ingredients:

2 cans pinto beans, drained
2 Cans White Beans, drained
2 cans chickpeas, drained
1 green bell pepper, diced
1 onion, chopped
2 tsp chili powder
2 cloves garlic
½ tsp oregano
4 cups vegetable broth

Directions:

Place all ingredients in the slow cooker and cook on low
for 4-6 hours.

Sweet and Spicy Chili

Ingredients:

2 cans pinto beans, drained
½ cup vegetable broth
1 can diced tomatoes and chili peppers
1 onion, chopped
1 can crushed tomatoes
2 cups black beans, cooked
½ tsp cumin
1 TBSP lime juice
2 TBSP hot sauce
¼ cup chopped cilantro
½ cup brown sugar

Directions:

Place all ingredients in the slow cooker and cook on low for 4 hours. Serve with additional cilantro as a garnish.

Autumn Pumpkin Soup

Ingredients:

16 oz Canned Pumpkin
1 yellow onion, diced
2 carrots, diced
1 gala apple, peeled, cored and diced
1 TBSP sage
1/3 cup coconut oil
3 cups vegetable broth
2 TBSP olive oil
¾ cup almond milk

Directions:

In a hot skillet, saute onions, carrots, apple, and sage in olive oil. When soft, place in a blender and puree until smooth. Pour into your slow cooker along with pumpkin, vegetable broth, and seasonings. Cook on low for 5 hours. Stir in coconut oil and almond milk. Cook on low for another hour.

Spinach Chickpea Soup

Ingredients:

2 Cups Fresh Baby Spinach Leaves
2 Cans Chickpeas
2-15 Ounce Cans Stewed Tomatoes
3 TBSP Paprika
1 tsp garlic
½ cup vegetable broth

Directions:

Place all ingredients in the slow cooker and stir to combine. Cook on low for 3-4 hours.

Vegan Split Pea Soup

Ingredients:

1 pound dried split peas
4 cups water
1 cup vegetable broth
1 cup extra firm tofu, drained and cubed
2 carrots, chopped
1 can of corn, drained
½ red bell pepper, chopped

Directions:

Combine all ingredients in a your slow cooker and stir.
Cover and cook on low for 8 hours.

Black Eyed Pea Stew

Ingredients:

2 cups dried black eyed peas
4 cups vegetable broth
4 cups water
6 carrots, peeled and chopped
½ cup chopped celery
½ cup chopped onion
2 cups spinach, chopped
Salt and pepper to taste

Directions:

Rinse and drain the black eyed peas and then place in the slow cooker. Add remaining ingredients and stir to combine. Cover and cook on low for 10 hours or until peas are tender.

Pumpkin Bisque

Ingredients:

30 oz. canned pumpkin pie filling
15 oz. canned pumpkin puree
28 oz. vegetable broth
½ cup water
¼ tsp Salt
¼ tsp pepper
1 cup coconut milk

Directions:

Combine all ingredients except coconut milk and cook on low for 4 hours. Add in coconut milk and stir. Cook for another 15 minutes.

Old Fashioned Vegetable Soup

Ingredients:

8 cups vegetable broth
1 can corn
1 can peas
2 carrots, chopped
2 celery stalks, chopped
1 onion, diced
1 potato, peeled and cut into ½ inch cubes
1 tsp parsley
1 tsp basil
Salt and pepper to taste

Directions:

Combine all ingredients in slow cooker and cook on low
for 6-8 hours or until potatoes are soft.

Apple Squash Bisque

Ingredients:

2 lb. butternut squash, peeled and cubed
1 yellow onion, chopped
2 cups vegetable broth
2 cups apple sauce
½ tsp ground ginger
¼ tsp salt
1 cup cashew cream

Directions:

Combine all ingredients except cashew cream in slow cooker and cook on low for 8-10 hours. Pour mixture into a blender and pulse until smooth. Pour back into slow cooker and add in cashew cream. Cook on low for another 15-20 minutes or until hot.

Last Minute Lentil Soup

Ingredients:

1 cup lentils, sorted and rinsed
4 cups vegetable stock
2 carrots, sliced
3 cloves garlic, minced
1 onion, diced
Salt and pepper to taste
1/2 tsp thyme

Directions:

Combine all ingredients in slow cooker and cook on low for 8-10 hours.

Indian Coconut Curry

Ingredients:

5 potatoes, peeled and cut into 1 inch cubes
¼ cup curry powder
2 TBSP flour
1 TBSP chili powder
½ tsp red pepper flakes
½ tsp cayenne pepper
1 green bell pepper, cut into strips
1 red bell pepper, cut into strips
1 packet onion soup mix
1 ½ cups coconut cream
1 ½ cups carrots, chopped
1 cup peas
¼ cup chopped cilantro
Water as needed

Directions:

Combine all ingredients except carrots and peas in the slow cooker. Cover and cook on low until the mixture is bubbling, adding water as needed to keep moist for 3 to 4 hours. Add the carrots and cook another 30 minutes. Stir the peas and cook until the vegetables are tender, about 30 minutes.

Squash and Black Bean Chili

Ingredients:

2 onions, chopped
4 cloves garlic, minced
1 red bell pepper, chopped
1 green bell pepper, chopped
2 jalapeno peppers, minced
4 cans black beans, rinsed and drained
2 cans diced tomatoes with liquid
3 TBSP chili powder
2 TBSP cumin
1 TBSP dried oregano
4 cups butternut squash, peeled and cut in ½ inch cubes)
Salt and pepper to taste

Directions:

Combine all ingredients in the slow cooker and cook on low for 8-10 hours or until squash is tender.

Five-Can Friday Soup

Ingredients:

1 (14 1/2 ounce) can diced tomatoes
1 (15 1/4 ounce) can corn
1 (15 ounce) can minestrone soup
1 (15 ounce) can mixed vegetables
1 (15 ounce) can black beans, rinsed

Directions:

Combine all ingredients in the slow cooker and cook on low 8-10 hours.

Cabbage Carrot Soup

Ingredients:

2 cups cabbage, chopped finely in strips
5 cups vegetable broth
Salt and pepper to taste
2 tsp parsley
2 -3 carrots, chopped finely in strips

Directions:

Combine all ingredients in slow cooker and cook on low
8-10 hours.

Tortellini Soup

Ingredients:

8 cups vegetable broth
fresh ground black pepper
2 (9 ounce) packages tortellini
2 cups diced tomatoes
2 TBSP chopped fresh Italian parsley

Directions:

Combine all ingredients in the slow cooker and cook on
low for 8 hours. Serve immediately.

Miso Soup

Ingredients:

2 cups water
2 cups vegetable broth
8 shiitake mushrooms, chopped
4 scallions
3 TBSP miso
3 ounce firm tofu, diced

Directions:

Combine all ingredients in the slow cooker. Cover and cook on low for 8-10 hours.

Cajun Gumbo

Ingredients:

2 cans black beans, rinsed and drained
1 can diced tomatoes, undrained
2 cans mixed vegetables, drained
2 cups frozen cut okra
3 tsp Cajun seasoning
2 cups vegetable broth

Directions:

Combine all ingredients in the slow cooker and cook on
low for 8 hours. Serve over white rice.

Sauerkraut and Apples

Ingredients:

1 pound sauerkraut
2 cups firm tofu, cubed
4 gala apples, chopped
½ cup raw honey
1 tsp Salt
¼ tsp pepper
½ tsp caraway seeds
¾ cup organic apple juice

Directions:

Rinse sauerkraut and squeeze dry. Place half of the sauerkraut in a slow cooker and layer tofu on top. Next, add apples, honey, seasonings, and caraway seeds. Add remainder of the sauerkraut on top and pour apple juice over the whole mixture. Cover and cook on low for 6-8 hours.

Maple Butternut Squash

Ingredients:

1 large butternut squash
1 cup organic apple juice
4 TBSP coconut oil, melted
¼ cup pure maple syrup
½ tsp cinnamon

Directions:

Pour the apple juice into the slow cooker. Combine the coconut oil, maple syrup, and cinnamon in a small bowl and set aside. Quarter the butternut squash lengthwise, cut stem off, and scoop out seeds. Put two of the squash quarters, cut side up, in the slow cooker. Drizzle with about half of the maple mixture. Place the remaining two squash quarters on the first ones and drizzle with remaining maple mixture. Cover and cook on low for 6 to 8 hours, or until squash is tender.

Cranberry Cabbage

Ingredients:

1 red cabbage, chopped
1 can cranberry sauce
1 onion, sliced
2 apples, peeled and chopped
½ cup organic apple juice
½ tsp thyme
½ tsp cinnamon
¼ tsp allspice
¼ tsp pepper
1 tsp salt
2 TBSP raw honey
4 TBSP red wine vinegar

Directions:

Place all ingredients in the slow cooker and stir to combine. Cook on low for 5-7 hours.

Southern Style Beets

Ingredients:

½ cup raw honey
¼ cup water
¼ cup white vinegar
2 cans whole beets, drained

Directions:

Combine ingredients in the slow cooker and cook on low for 6-8 hours.

Summer Zucchini

Ingredients:

4 TBSP coconut oil
1 onion, sliced
1 cucumber, seeded and sliced
2 large zucchini, sliced
1 green bell pepper, julienned
1 red bell pepper, julienned
½ cup apple cider
Salt and pepper to taste

Directions:

Combine all ingredients in the slow cooker and cook on low for 4-6 hours or until vegetables are tender.

Greek Style Eggplant

Ingredients:

1 large eggplant, cut into 1-inch cubes
2 onions, sliced
2 celery stalks, sliced
1 TBSP olive oil
2 cans dice tomatoes with liquid
3 TBSP tomato sauce
½ cup olives, pitted and halved
2 TBSP balsamic vinegar
1 TBSP honey
1 tsp oregano
Salt and pepper to taste

Directions:

Add all ingredients to the slow cooker and stir to combine. Cook on low for 4-5 hours or until eggplant is tender.

Dinner Vegetable Medley

Ingredients:

1 medium cabbage, chopped
1 small rutabaga, cut in chunks
3 stalks of celery, chopped
2 dozen baby carrots
2 medium onions, cut in chunks
1 tsp onion powder
1 can diced tomatoes
1 can organic vegetable juice

Directions:

Combine all ingredients in the slow cooker and cover. Cook on low for 4-6 hours and serve.

Italian Stewed Tomatoes

Ingredients:

7 or 8 ripe tomatoes, diced
2 TBSP coconut oil
1 medium onion, sliced
¾ cup chopped celery
½ cup bell pepper, chopped
3 TBSP raw honey
1 tsp parsley
1/8 tsp pepper
1 tsp Salt

Directions:

Combine all ingredients in the slow cooker and stir. Cover and cook on low for 8-10 hours. Serve over rice.

Slow Cooked Artichokes

Ingredients:

5 artichokes, stalks removed

1 ½ tsp Salt

8 peppercorns

2 stalks celery, sliced

1 lemon, cut into rounds

2 cups water

Directions:

Combine all ingredients in the slow cooker and cook on low for 4-6 hours.

Stuffed Peppers

Ingredients:

4 large green bell peppers
1 cup steamed cauliflower, mashed
1 cup whole kernel corn
1 cup olives, pits removed and cut in half
½ cup chives
¼ tsp sea Salt
¼ tsp garlic pepper
1 can diced tomatoes with liquid
1/3 cup red wine vinegar
1 can tomato paste

Directions:

Cut tops off peppers and scoop out seeds and inner ribs. Remove the stems from the tops and cut up remaining pepper pieces. Add pepper pieces to a mixing bowl with steamed cauliflower, corn, olives, chives, ½ diced tomatoes, and seasonings. Mix together and stuff the peppers, packing lightly. Stand the peppers upright in your slow cooker. In a separate bowl, combine remaining tomatoes with their liquid, vinegar, and tomato paste and stir. Pour mixture over and around the peppers in the slow cooker.

Cover and cook on low for 5-6 hours until peppers are tender, but still hold their shape.

Barbecue Tofu

Ingredients:

2 containers firm or extra firm tofu, pressed
1 1/2 cups ketchup
3 TBSP brown sugar
2 TBSP soy sauce
1 TBSP apple cider vinegar
1 TBSP red pepper flakes
1/2 tsp garlic powder
Salt and pepper to taste

Directions:

Combine all ingredients in a slow cooker. Cover and cook on low for 5-6 hours.

Teriyaki Tofu

Ingredients:

2 containers firm or extra firm tofu, pressed
1 1/2 cups teriyaki sauce
1 TBSP apple cider vinegar
1/2 tsp garlic powder
Salt and pepper to taste

Directions:

Combine all ingredients in a slow cooker. Cover and cook on low for 5-6 hours.

White Beans and Sun Dried Tomatoes

Ingredients:

2 cups Great Northern beans
3 cloves garlic, minced
1 onion, chopped
3 cups vegetable broth
3 cups water
1 tsp Salt
1/2 tsp Italian seasoning
3/4 cup chopped sun dried tomatoes in oil, drained
4 ounce can sliced black olives, drained
1 cup shredded cheese substitute

Directions:

Combine all ingredients in the slow cooker except tomatoes, olives, and cheese substitute. Cover and cook on low 4-6 hours or until beans are tender. Stir in tomatoes, olives, and cheese substitute and cover. Cook for an additional hour.

Slow Cooker Ravioli

Ingredients:

1 onion, chopped
3 cloves garlic, minced
4 cups marinara sauce
8 oz. can tomato sauce
1 (14-ounce) can diced tomatoes, undrained
4 (9 oz.) packages of refrigerated vegan ravioli
2 cups shredded cheese substitute

Directions:

Place onion and garlic in bottom of 4-6 quart slow cooker. Add spaghetti sauce, tomato sauce, and undrained tomatoes and stir well. Cover and cook on low for 8-9 hours until onion is tender. Turn heat to high and stir in refrigerated ravioli. Cover and cook on high for 1 hour longer; then sprinkle with cheese substitute and cook for 5-10 minutes until ravioli is tender.

Three Bean Italian Cassoulet

Ingredients:

1 cup dried lima beans
1 cup dried great Northern beans
1 cup dried garbanzo beans
4-1/2 cups water
16 oz. bag baby carrots
1 onion, chopped
3 garlic cloves, minced
2 TBSP Italian seasoning
1/2 tsp Salt
1/8 tsp white pepper
1 bay leaf
14 oz. can diced tomatoes, undrained
2 TBSP tomato paste

Directions:

Soak beans overnight and drain. Combine beans, 4-1/2 cups water, carrots, onion, garlic and seasonings except Salt, tomatoes, and tomato paste in 3-1/2 to 4 quart slow cooker. Mix well to combine. Cover and cook on high for 30 minutes. Reduce heat to low and cook for 8-9 hours or until beans and vegetables are tender. Stir in tomatoes, tomato paste, and Salt, cover, and cook 1 hour longer on low. Remove bay leaf before serving.

Barley Casserole

Ingredients:

1 TBSP olive oil
1 yellow onion, chopped
3 cloves garlic, minced
1 cup uncooked pearl barley
½ cup tomato juice
½ tsp thyme
½ tsp oregano
¼ tsp salt
¼ tsp pepper
1 red bell pepper, chopped
1 cup chopped mushrooms
2-1/2 cups vegetable broth
1/3 cup toasted pine nuts

Directions:

Saute onion and garlic in olive oil until tender. Then combine all ingredients except pine nuts in a 3-quart slow cooker. Cover and cook on low for 6-8 hours until barley and vegetables are tender. Sprinkle with nuts just before serving.

Meatless Sloppy Joes

Ingredients:

1 cup lentils, soaked overnight
2 cups water
2 onions, chopped
3 carrots, chopped
4 stalks celery, chopped
3/4 cup ketchup
3 TBSP brown sugar
1 TBSP cider vinegar
1 TBSP yellow mustard
1 tsp Italian seasoning
10 sandwich rolls, split and toasted

Directions:

Combine all ingredients except for vinegar, mustard, and sandwich rolls. Place in the slow cooker and cover. Cook on low for 8-12 hours or until lentils are tender. Stir in vinegar and mustard just before serving. Make sandwiches using toasted buns.

Southern Chickpeas and Grits

Ingredients:

1 green bell pepper, chopped
4 cloves garlic, minced
3 cups cooked chickpeas
1 cup water
3 cups diced tomatoes
1 tsp chipotle powder
3-4 dashes of liquid smoke
3-4 dashes of hot sauce
Salt and pepper to taste

Directions:

Combine all ingredients in the slow cooker and cook on low for 6-8 hours. Serve over a warm bowl of grits.

Lemon Pepper Tofu

Ingredients:

2 containers firm or extra firm tofu, pressed
3 TBSP brown sugar
2 TBSP soy sauce
1 TBSP apple cider vinegar
1 TBSP red pepper flakes
1/2 tsp garlic powder
1 ½ tsp lemon pepper
Juice from 1 lemon
Salt and pepper to taste

Directions:

Combine all ingredients in a slow cooker. Cover and
cook on low for 5-6 hours.

No Beans Refried Beans

Ingredients:

2 medium butternut squash, peeled, seeded, and diced
1 cup sun dried tomatoes
1 TBSP tomato paste
1 cup water
2 tsp cumin
1 tsp cayenne
1 tsp chili powder
1 tsp garlic
Salt and pepper to taste

Directions:

Soak the tomatoes in water for half an hour. Place the tomatoes in the slow cooker and add in squash, tomato paste, sun dried tomatoes, and water. Sprinkle spices on top and stir. Cook on low for 3 hours. Use a potato masher to create the consistency of refried beans.

Carrot Pudding

Ingredients:

4 large carrots, grated
1 small onion, grated
1/2 tsp Salt
1/4 tsp nutmeg
1 TBSP raw honey
1 cup almond milk
1 ½ bananas, pureed

Directions:

Mix together the carrots, onion, Salt, nutmeg, sugar, milk, and bananas. Pour into greased slow cooker; cover and cook on high for 3-4 hours.

Orange Pecan Carrots

Ingredients:

3 cups sliced carrots
3 TBSP coconut oil
2 cups water
3 TBSP organic orange jam
¼ tsp Salt
1/8 cup chopped pecans

Directions:

Combine all ingredients in the slow cooker and cover. Cook on low for 4-6 hours or until tender.

German Cole Slaw

Ingredients:

1 head cabbage, shredded
1 large onion, chopped
2 green peppers, chopped
1 tsp celery seed
1 ½ cups white vinegar
1 ½ tsp mustard seed
1 tsp turmeric
1 tsp salt

Directions:

Combine all ingredients in the slow cooker and stir to make sure everything is thoroughly mixed. Cover and cook on low for 4-5 hours. Pour into a bowl and chill in refrigerator for at least 1 hour before serving.

Cauliflower Mash

Ingredients:

1 head of cauliflower, chopped
1 cup vegetable broth
2 TBSP coconut oil
Salt and pepper to taste

Directions:

Add cauliflower, vegetable broth, and coconut oil to slow cooker. Cook on low for 4 hours or until cauliflower is soft. Use a potato masher to mash cauliflower well and add salt and pepper to taste.

Brocolli with Toasted Hazelnuts

Ingredients:

2 lbs. broccoli florets
1 cup of hazelnuts
1 TBSP olive oil
Juice from 2 lemons
½ tsp salt
½ tsp pepper

Directions:

Combine all ingredients in the slow cooker and toss to combine. Cover and cook on low for 4-5 hours or until broccoli reaches desired consistency.

Teriyaki Broccoli and Mushrooms

Ingredients:

2 cups broccoli florets
2 cups mushrooms, sliced
½ cup teriyaki sauce
½ cup pineapple juice
1 TBSP olive oil
½ tsp salt
½ tsp pepper

Directions:

Combine all ingredients in the slow cooker and toss to combine. Cover and cook on low for 4-5 hours or until broccoli reaches desired consistency.

Honey Dijon Brussels Sprouts

Ingredients:

1 pound Brussels sprouts
3 TBSP olive oil
1 TBSP Dijon mustard
¼ tsp salt
¼ tsp pepper
¼ cup water

Directions:

Combine all ingredients in the slow cooker and toss to combine. Cover and cook on low for 4-5 hours or until brussels sprouts reach desired consistency.

Lemon Pepper Brussels Sprouts

Ingredients:

1 pound Brussels sprouts
3 TBSP olive oil
Juice from 2 lemons
¼ tsp Salt
1 tsp lemon pepper
¼ cup water

Directions:

Combine all ingredients in the slow cooker and toss to combine. Cover and cook on low for 4-5 hours or until brussels sprouts reach desired consistency.

Garlic Lemon Asparagus

Ingredients:

1 pound asparagus spears, ends trimmed off
2 cloves garlic, minced
Juice from 1 lemon
1 TBSP olive oil
Salt and pepper to taste

Directions:

Combine all ingredients in the slow cooker and toss to combine. Cover and cook on low for around 2 hours or until tender crisp.

Winter Root Vegetable Medley

Ingredients:

2 pounds carrots
2 pounds rutabagas
2 pounds parsnips
½ cup chopped parsley
3 TBSP olive oil
1 tsp salt
1 tsp pepper
1 tsp basil

Directions:

Peel all the vegetables and cut into bite size chunks. Then toss into the slow cooker and combine with remaining ingredients. Cover and cook on low for 8-9 hours.

Smashed Turnips

Ingredients:

4 turnips, peeled and quartered
4 potatoes, peeled and quartered
2 TBSP minced onion
1 ½ tsp Salt, divided
water
¼ cup cashew cream
2 TBSP olive oil
1/8 tsp pepper

Directions:

Combine turnips, potatoes, onions and 1 tsp of the Salt in the bottom of a slow cooker. Add water to cover. Cover slow cooker and cook on low for 6-8 hours. Drain. Mash the mixture with a potato masher. Stir in remaining ingredients and continuing mashing until smooth.

Baked Sweet Potatoes

Ingredients:

5-6 Medium Sweet Potatoes
Salt and Pepper to taste

Directions:

Wash sweet potatoes well but don't dry. Put on the bottom of the crock pot, put lid on, and turn on low. Cook for 6-8 hours or until tender. Serve with salt and pepper to taste.

Caramel Glazed Sweet Potatoes

Ingredients:

4 to 6 medium sweet potatoes, peeled and sliced
1 cup brown sugar
3 TBSP cornstarch
1 tsp cinnamon
½ tsp salt
2 TBSP vegan butter spread

Directions:

Grease the slow cooker and add sliced sweet potatoes and sprinkle with Salt. Combine sugar, cornstarch and cinnamon; sprinkle over the sweet potatoes. Dot with Vegan butter spread; cover and cook on low for 7 to 9 hours.

Slow Cooker Corn on the Cob

Ingredients:

8 ears of corn
Olive Oil
Salt and pepper to taste

Directions:

Drizzle each ear of corn with olive oil and sprinkle on Salt and pepper. Wrap in aluminum foil and place in the slow cooker. Once all ears are in the slow cooker, cover and cook on low for 4-5 hours or until corn is tender crisp.

Summer Garlic Green Beans

Ingredients:

1 pound green beans, washed and trimmed
2 TBSP olive oil
1 tsp Salt
¼ tsp pepper
3 cloves garlic, minced
1 cup vegetable broth

Directions:

Combine all ingredients in the slow cooker and toss to combine. Cover and cook on low for around 2 hours or until tender crisp.

Fast and Easy Slow Cooker Rice

Ingredients:

1 cup rice
2 cups water
Salt to taste
2 tsp olive oil

Directions:

Grease the slow cooker and pour in rice and water. Cover and cook on high for 1 ½ to 2 ½ hours, stirring occasionally.

Cajun Beans and Rice

Ingredients:

3 cups cooked beans
1 cup brown rice
1 cup vegetable broth
1 can of diced tomatoes
1 TBSP coconut oil, melted
1 tsp cumin
½ tsp garlic powder
2 cups water
½ cup Diced green chilies
Hot sauce or cayenne pepper to taste
Salt and pepper to taste

Directions:

Grease the slow cooker and pour in all ingredients. Cover and cook on high for 1 ½ to 2 ½ hours, stirring occasionally.

Sweet Pineapple Baked Beans

Ingredients:

2 cans pinto beans
1 8 ounce can pineapple chunks, drained
1 onion, diced
2 cloves garlic, minced
1/2 cup barbecue sauce
2 TBSP maple syrup
1 TBSP soy sauce
Salt and pepper to taste

Directions:

Combine all ingredients in the slow cooker and toss to combine. Cover and cook on low for around 6-8 hours.

Scalloped Potatoes

Ingredients:

1/2 onion, diced
2 cloves garlic, minced
1 TBSP parsley
1 tsp Salt
Pepper to taste
7-8 potatoes, sliced thin
8 oz Tofutti cream cheese substitute

Directions:

Lightly grease a slow cooker. In a small bowl, combine the onion, garlic, parsley, Salt, and pepper. Place a layer of the sliced potatoes on the bottom of the slow cooker. Sprinkle with some of the onion and garlic mix. Top with 1/3 of the Tofutti. Continue layering potatoes, spices and cream cheese. Sprinkle the top with additional Salt and pepper. Cover and cook on high for 3-4 hours, or until potatoes are done cooking.

Vegan Slow Cooker Fudge

Ingredients:

2 ½ cups Vegan chocolate chips
½ cup canned coconut milk
¼ cup honey
1/8 tsp Salt
1 tsp pure vanilla extract
Coconut oil

Directions:

Grease the slow cooker with coconut oil. In a bowl, stir together all ingredients except vanilla and then pour into the slow cooker. Cook on high for 2 hours. Uncover and turn off heat; stir in vanilla extract. Then leave the mixture uncovered in the slow cooker (turned off) for 3-4 hours until it's room temperature. When it reaches room temperature, stir for 10 minutes and then pour into a well-greased container and cool in the fridge overnight.

Bananas Foster

Ingredients:

4 bananas, medium firmness
1 TBSP coconut oil
1 TBSP lemon juice
3 TBSP raw honey
1 tsp cinnamon
½ tsp nutmeg
½ tsp cloves

Directions:

Combine all ingredients except bananas into slow cooker and turn on high for 5-10 minutes or until melted. Stir together and then reduce slow cooker heat to low. Slice bananas to ¼ inch thick and add them in the slow cooker. Toss to combine with honey mixture. Cook on low for 2 hours.

Honey Glazed Pears

Ingredients:

4 pears, halved and cored
1 TBSP lemon juice
1 cup raw honey
2 TBSp coconut oil, melted
¼ cup water
½ tsp pure vanilla extra
1 tsp cinnamon

Directions:

Place pears in your slow cooker and top with remaining ingredients. Stir together gently to combine. Cover and cook on low for 4-6 hours or until pears are fork tender.

Southern Cherry Jubilee

Ingredients:

2 TBSP melted coconut oil
4 cups black cherries, pitted
1 cup raw honey
Zest from ½ lemon
1 cup water
½ tsp cinnamon

Directions:

Combine all ingredients in a slow cooker and cover. Cook on low for 3-4 hours. Serve with whipped coconut cream if desired.

Walnut Strawberry Surprise

Ingredients:

3 cups fresh strawberries, capped and quartered
½ cup honey
1 tsp cinnamon
1 tsp pure maple syrup
½ cup walnuts, chopped
1 cup water
Zest from ½ lemon

Directions:

Combine all ingredients in your slow cooker and toss to mix. Cover and cook on low for 3-4 hours.

Hawaiian Tapioca Pudding

Ingredients:

¾ cup raw honey
1 cup small pearl tapioca
3 cups coconut milk
1 egg
½ cup coconut
½ cup chopped pineapple

Directions:

Combine all ingredients and pour into a well greased slow cooker. Cover and cook on low for 4 hours.

Berry Mint Medley

Ingredients:

1 cup blackberries
1 cup blueberries
1 cup raspberries
½ cup raw honey
½ cup coconut milk
1 tsp allspice
Small handful fresh mint, chopped

Directions:

Combine all ingredients except for mint in the slow cooker. Stir and cover. Cook on low for 2 hours. Add in mint leaves and cook for another 30 minutes.

Chocolate Peanut Butter Cake

Ingredients:

Cake:
1 cup flour
½ cup sugar
2 TBSP cocoa powder
1 ½ tsp baking powder
½ cup soy milk
2 TBSP coconut oil, melted
1 tsp vanilla
¾ cup vegan chocolate chips

Peanut Butter Layer:
¾ cup sugar
¼ cup cocoa powder
1 cup boiling water
½ cup peanut butter

Directions:

Grease the slow cooker. In a mixing bowl, combine the cake ingredients and mix until smooth. Pour into the prepared slow cooker. In a mixing bowl, combine the sugar and cocoa powder.

In a separate bowl, combine the boiling water and the peanut butter. Mix into the cocoa mixture.

Carefully pour evenly over the cake batter. Cover and cook on high for 2 to 2 ½ hours, until a toothpick inserted into the center comes out clean.

Simple Rice Pudding

Ingredients:

4 cups vanilla soy milk
1 cup uncooked rice
1 cup sugar
3 TBSP Vegan margarine
Pinch of Salt
1 tsp vanilla
¼ cup dried cranberries
¼ cup raisins
½ tsp cinnamon

Directions:

Combine all the ingredients in a slow cooker. Cook on low for 2 to 4 hours, stirring every hour, until the desired consistency is reached.

Slow Cooker Apple Cobbler

Ingredients:

4 ½ cups granny smith apples, peeled, cored, and sliced
2 TBSP flour
1/3 cup white sugar
¾ cup brown sugar
1/3 cup dried cranberries
¼ tsp cinnamon
2/3 cup oats
1 cup water
3 TBSP melted Vegan margarine

Directions:

In a mixing bowl, toss the apples in the flour and white sugar to coat. Stir in the dried cranberries, cinnamon, and oats. Pour the water into a slow cooker and add the apple mixture. Pour the melted Vegan margarine over the apples and sprinkle with the brown sugar. Cover and cook on low for 4 to 6 hours, or until the apples are tender.

Georgia Peach Cobbler

Ingredients:

4 ½ cups sliced peaches
2 TBSP flour
1/3 cup white sugar
¾ cup brown sugar
½ tsp cinnamon
2/3 cup oats
1 cup water
3 TBSP melted Vegan margarine

Directions:

In a mixing bowl, toss the peaches in the flour and white sugar to coat. Stir in the cinnamon and oats. Pour the water into a slow cooker and add the peach mixture. Pour the melted Vegan margarine over the apples and sprinkle with the brown sugar. Cover and cook on low for 4 to 6 hours, or until the peaches are tender.

Crustless Pumpkin Pie

Ingredients:

15-oz. can pumpkin
1 1/3 cups nondairy creamer
½ cup sugar
¼ cup brown sugar
½ cup Bisquick
Egg replacer equivalent to 2 eggs
2 TBSP melted Vegan margarine
2 ½ tsp pumpkin pie spice
2 tsp vanilla

Directions:

Combine all ingredients in a bowl and pour into a greased slow cooker. Cook on low for 7-8 hours.

Apple Pudding Can Cake

Ingredients:

2 cups sugar
1 cup vegetable oil
Egg replacer equivalent to 2 eggs
2 tsp vanilla
2 cups flour
1 tsp baking soda
1 tsp nutmeg
2 cups unpeeled apple, finely chopped
1 cup chopped nuts (walnuts or pecans)

Directions:

Beat together sugar, oil, egg substitute, and vanilla. Add apple with dry ingredients and mix well. Take a 2-pound tin can and grease well. Pour the cake batter into can, filling no more than 2/3 full. Place the can in your slow cooker and cover, but leave a gap for steam to escape. Cook on high for 3 ½ to 4 hours. Cake is done when the top is set.

Cherry Cobbler

Ingredients:

1 can cherry pie filling
2/3 cup brown sugar
½ cup quick-cooking oats
½ cup flour
1 tsp brown sugar
1/3 Vegan margarine butter, softened

Directions:

Grease the slow cooker and place cherry pie filling in the bottom. Combine dry ingredients in a mixing bowl and cut in margarine with a pastry cutter. Sprinkle crumbs over cherry filling. Cover and cook on low for 5 hours.

Simple Marinara Sauce

Ingredients:

2 (28 oz.) cans crushed tomatoes
1 (6 oz.) can tomato paste
1 medium yellow onion, chopped
½ TBSP minced garlic
2 whole bay leaves
1 TBSP Italian seasoning
1 TBSP brown sugar
1 TBSP balsamic vinegar
Salt and pepper to taste

Directions:

Combine all ingredients in the slow cooker and cover. Cook on low for 8-10 hours.

Chunky Spaghetti Sauce

Ingredients:

2 (28 oz.) cans crushed tomatoes
1 (6 oz.) can tomato paste
2 medium yellow onions, chopped
1 green bell pepper, chopped
1 red bell pepper, chopped
1 cup mushrooms, chopped
½ TBSP minced garlic
2 whole bay leaves
1 TBSP Italian seasoning
1 TBSP brown sugar
1 TBSP balsamic vinegar
Salt and pepper to taste

Directions:

Combine all ingredients in the slow cooker and cover.
Cook on low for 8-10 hours.

Vegan Alfredo Sauce

Ingredients:

2 cups canned coconut milk
1 cup nutritional yeast
2 cloves garlic, minced
2 tsp basil
2 tsp sea Salt
1 tsp black pepper

Directions:

Mix together all ingredients and pour in the slow cooker. Heat on low for 2-3 hours, stirring occasionally.

Citrus Luau Sauce

Ingredients:

2 cups pineapple juice
½ cup orange juice
Zest from ½ orange
½ cup soy sauce
1 clove of garlic, minced
2 tsp red wine vinegar
2 TBSP cornstarch

Directions:

Combine ingredients in the slow cooker and cover. Cook on low for 1-2 hours. Serve as a dressing over a warm vegetable medley.

Triple Threat Hot Sauce

Ingredients:

2 cups chopped tomatoes
5 jalapeno peppers, diced
2 serrano peppers, diced
1 habanero pepper, diced
1 yellow onion, chopped
1 cup white vinegar
½ cup pineapple sauce
5 cloves garlic, minced
1 cup water
Salt and pepper to taste

Directions:

Combine all ingredients and cook on low for 8 hours. Pour mixture into a blender and puree until smooth. Serve as a veggie dipping sauce or use as a super spicy marinade.

Cranberry Sauce

Ingredients:

1 package of fresh cranberries (12 oz)
½ cup orange juice
½ cup water
½ cup brown sugar
½ cup white sugar
¼ tsp cinnamon

Directions:

Combine ingredients in the slow cooker and cover. Cook on high for 3-4 hours or until cranberries pop.

Dijon Barbecue Sauce

Ingredients:

4 cups ketchup
1 yellow onion, chopped
¼ cup brown sugar
1 TBSP celery Salt
2 TBSP ground mustard
½ cup water
2 TBSP Worcestershire sauce
2 TBSP prepared yellow mustard
2 TBSP molasses
1 TBSP cider vinegar
4 tsp paprika
Salt and pepper to taste

Directions:

Combine all ingredients in the slow cooker and cook on low for 6-8 hours, stirring occasionally.

Memphis Sweet Barbecue Sauce

Ingredients:

4 cups ketchup
2 cups brown sugar
1 yellow onion, chopped
1 TBSP celery Salt
2 TBSP ground mustard
½ cup water
2 TBSP Worcestershire sauce
2 TBSP molasses
½ TBSP cider vinegar
3 tsp paprika
Salt and pepper to taste

Directions:

Combine all ingredients in the slow cooker and cook on low for 6-8 hours, stirring occasionally.

Pineapple Caribbean Jerk Glaze

Ingredients:

3 TBSP Vegan margarine
2 TBSP chives
1 cup water
1 cup ketchup
2 TBSP white vinegar
2 TBSP hot sauce
2 tsp pepper
2 tsp Worcestershire sauce
2 tsp lemon juice
2 tsp cayenne pepper
2 tsp Italian seasoning
½ cup pineapple juice
½ tsp cinnamon
½ tsp garlic powder
Salt and pepper to taste

Directions:

Combine all ingredients in the slow cooker and cook on low for 6-8 hours, stirring occasionally.

Sweet Mango Salsa

Ingredients:

1 can mandarin oranges, chopped
2 large ripe mangos, peeled, pitted, cut into 1/4-inch pieces
1/2 cup flaked sweetened coconut
1/2 cup chopped red onion
1/2 cup chopped fresh cilantro
2 jalapenos, chopped
Juice from 1 lime
1 tsp cayenne pepper
1 cup diced tomatoes

Directions:

Combine all ingredients in the slow cooker and cover. Cook on low for 6-8 hours, stirring occasionally.

Pumpkin Butter

Ingredients:

1 15-ounce can pumpkin
½ cup apple juice
¾ cup granulated sugar
1 tsp ground cinnamon
¼ tsp ground ginger
¼ tsp ground nutmeg
1/8 tsp cloves

Directions:

Combine all ingredients in the slow cooker and cover. Cook on low for 6-8 hours, stirring occasionally. Chill in the refrigerator overnight before serving.

Apple Butter

Ingredients:

8-10 apples- peeled, cored, and chopped or sliced

¾ cup of apple juice

1 ½ cups of brown sugar

1/8 tsp nutmeg

½ tsp ground cloves

¼ tsp allspice

3 whole cinnamon sticks

Directions:

Combine ingredients in the slow cooker and cook on low for 6-8 hours. Remove cinnamon sticks and pour mixture into a blender. Pulse until you achieve a smooth consistency. Chill in the refrigerator before serving.

Slow Cooker Strawberry Jam

Ingredients:

4 pints fresh strawberries, capped and sliced
2 TBSP lemon juice
4 cups sugar
1 (1.75 Oz.) package powdered fruit pectin

Directions:

Place all ingredients in the slow cooker and stir to combine. Cover and cook on low for 1 hour. Stir well and continue cooking for one more hour. Increase heat to high and cook additional 2-3 hours until jam reaches desired consistency. Store jam in the refrigerator for up to 2 months or in the freezer for up to 1 year.

Printed in Great Britain
by Amazon.co.uk, Ltd.,
Marston Gate.